PROPERT'
ST. NICHOLAS S`H _ _ _ _
LOS AL OS HILLS

ST NICHOLAS CATHOLIC SCHOOL

W9-CQW-989

St. Nicholas School Library
12816 S. El Monte, Los Altos Hills, CA 94022
650-941-4056

# GULLS

PROPERTY OF
ST. NICHOLAS SCHOOL LIBRARY
LOS ALTOS HILLS

# GULLS

by *Sarel Eimerl*

PROPERTY OF
ST. NICH⋯ ⋯⋯ LIBRARY
LOS ALTOS HILLS

598.2
Eim

*Simon and Schuster* · *New York*

*All rights reserved*
*including the right of reproduction*
*in whole or in part in any form*

*Text copyright ©️ 1969 by Sarel Eimerl*

*Published by Simon and Schuster, Children's Book Division*
*Rockefeller Center, 630 Fifth Avenue*
*New York, New York 10020*

*First Printing*

*SBN 671–65078–5 Trade*
*SBN 671–65079–3 Library*
*Library of Congress Catalog Card Number: 76-86944*

*Manufactured in the United States of America*
*Printed by Pearl Pressman Liberty Incorporated, Philadelphia, Pa.*

PHOTOGRAPH CREDITS

*Cover, p. 12(b)   Alfred M. Baily*
*from National Audubon Society*
*pp. 6–7   H. W. Kitchen*
*from National Audubon Society*
*pp. 8–9, 13, 22, 28, 39, 40–41*
*Allan D. Cruickshank*
*from National Audubon Society*
*p. 10   M. F. Soper*
*from National Audubon Society*
*pp. 3, 4, 12(t), 18, 21, 26, 34, 36,*
*43, 46, 47*
*Gordon S. Smith from*
*National Audubon Society*
*p. 14   Robert C. Hermes*
*p. 15   Frank Stevens*
*from National Audubon Society*
*p. 19   Anthony Mercieca*
*from National Audubon Society*
*pp. 16–17   Ray Hunold*
*from National Audubon Society*
*p. 24   Henry Kyllingstad*
*from National Audubon Society*
*p. 38   Louis Quitt*
*from National Audubon Society*
*p. 31   Ed Park*
*from National Audubon Society*
*p. 32   Karl W. Kenyon*
*from National Audubon Society*
*pp. 37, 51   Eric Hosking*
*from National Audubon Society*
*p. 54   Arthur Swoger*
*from National Audubon Society*

*California Gulls and white pelicans nest at Lake Bowdoin National Wildlife Refuge in Montana.*

PART ONE

*One of the largest gulls is the Southern Blackbacked Gull.*

If you have ever been to the seashore, you must have seen gulls. There are gulls on practically every beach all over the world.

But gulls live not only on beaches. Some live on islands, such as the Canary Islands, which lie far out in the Atlantic Ocean. Others live around the shores of great inland lakes, like Lake Huron, or Great Salt Lake in Utah. There are even gulls that live in marshes amid the spreading prairies of North Dakota. However, most gulls live near the sea.

Herring Gulls are the most common kind of gull.

Dusky Gulls were photographed on the Galapagos Islands.

There are about forty different kinds. The smallest, called the Little Gull, measures only eleven inches from its head to its tail. The two biggest, the Glaucous and the Great Blackback, are almost three times as long.

All gulls, big and small alike, have long wings and heavy bodies. They also possess long, stout bills that curve downward and end with a sharp hook at the tip.

*Another large gull, the Glaucous Gull, is nearly three feet from head to tail.*

*Terns belong to the same family as gulls but are usually smaller and have straight bills.*

They belong to the same family as another group of seabirds called terns. However, most terns are smaller than gulls. Their bodies are more slender and their bills are straight.

There are many more gulls than terns. In fact gulls are the most common of all seabirds. You may wonder why, for they don't look especially tough or dangerous. In a way, you might say gulls are lucky. Many

PROPERTY OF
ST. NICHOLAS SCHOOL LIBRARY
LOS ALTOS HILLS

birds can eat only one kind of food. Some eat only insects. Others eat only fish. Or snails. Or seeds. But gulls can eat practically anything they can swallow.

They eat insects and mice and moles. They eat dead cats and rats. They are especially fond of shellfish, such as oysters and clams. They pick up fish that are washed ashore by the waves. They steal eggs belonging to other birds.

*Gulls can eat nearly anything. This one has found a starfish.*

*Gulls may follow a ship for hours waiting for scraps.*

*Here, a flock lands on a garbage scow.*

*A Ring-billed Gull hovers, watching for food.*

The bigger gulls even attack wounded birds, and kill and eat them. Occasionally, gulls also chase and catch live prey. When doing so, they can be tremendously fast and agile. Watch a gull sometime as it cruises over the water. It may look as if it is just flying lazily around, the way a human being walks when he is out for a stroll. But its eyes are fixed on the water, searching for fish just under the surface.

Suddenly it spots one. Very quickly, it turns in mid-air and swoops down. With its wings flapping hard, it races low over the water. Then it plunges just under the surface and grabs the fish in its long bill.

Or you may notice a gull that seems to hang in the air without moving. This is called hovering, and it is a big help to gulls in catching their prey.

Suppose a gull is flying over land and spots a rabbit. He swoops down to attack. Rabbits can run very quickly and this one gets away. It reaches the hole that leads to its home under the ground. But the danger is not over. Now the gull knows there are rabbits under that particular piece of ground. Silently, scarcely moving, he hovers in the air above the hole. Sooner or later a rabbit will come out.

*Spying a fish, a gull plunges down and catches it.*

Before the rabbit can spot the danger, the gull swoops and grabs it. He does not need to kill the rabbit right away. For a big gull is strong enough to fly quite a distance while holding a rabbit in his bill, to escape from hawks or other gulls.

The big gulls are also great thieves. They often settle near smaller birds which are searching or diving for fish. As soon as a small bird makes a catch, the gull races in and seizes it. Sometimes he will also kill and eat the other bird.

The Herring Gull is especially good at seizing food from other birds. It is about twenty-four inches long, and the gull that you most often see at the beach. It will often chase a bird that is carrying a fish or a stolen egg home to eat. The Herring Gull keeps attacking the other bird until it drops the egg or the fish. Of course the egg will break if it hits the ground. But Herring Gulls are so fast and agile they can sometimes catch an egg in mid-air.

Most creatures that hunt for food are able to move very quickly. They must also have plenty of patience, for they often spend lots of time searching for prey. Gulls, too, are patient and not only when hunting.

*Gulls live together in large flocks sometimes containing over a thousand birds.*

Red legs and beak and unusual feather markings belong to the Franklin's Gull of Utah and the Great Plains.

They may follow a ship for hours, or even days. They are waiting for food to be thrown overboard. Herring Gulls are especially patient when they are trying to crack shellfish, such as oysters and clams, to get at the meat inside. The shells are much too tough for humans to crack, either with their fingers or teeth. Gulls can't crack the shells in their bills, either, and they don't try.

If a gull picks up a clam on the beach, he simply carries it high in the air and then drops it. The clam may land on the wet sand or on a rock, and the shell will break open. But what if the shell falls into the water, or onto a soft area of sand? Then it doesn't break. The gull does not give up. He carries the clam back into the air and drops it again. He may drop the same shellfish a dozen times before it lands in the right place and breaks open.

The easiest way to recognize different kinds of gulls is by their coloring. The backs and wings of most adult gulls are white or gray or black. But their bills and legs and wing tips can be of many different colors.

The Herring Gull has a yellow bill and black wing tips with white spots. The Kittiwake, which often lives far out at sea, has a yellow bill and black legs.

*Kittiwakes nest on a rocky cliff on Egg Island, Alaska.*

Many Franklin's Gulls live on the Great Plains of the Midwest, or near Salt Lake City. They have red bills and legs.

All young gulls have their own special coloring. An adult Herring Gull is mostly gray. So is an adult Kittiwake. But a baby Herring Gull is part yellow and part white. A baby Kittiwake is a mixture of white and yellowish gray.

These gull chicks soon change color. Every spring and fall their old feathers drop out. They are replaced by new feathers of a different color. So the young gulls' color keeps changing.

During this time it is possible to tell a gull's age just by looking at its feathers. But after two years, most gulls have taken on their adult coloring. After gulls are grown, their old feathers drop out and are replaced twice a year, spring and fall, but their color remains the same.

Despite all their differences, most gulls have the same kinds of habits. To begin with, they live in large groups. A single group may contain several thousand birds. Every new chick belongs to the same group as its father and mother. It stays in that group always.

About two out of every four gull chicks die before they are a year old. It is unlikely that many of them live to be more than ten. Herring Gulls live the longest, and one is known to have lived twenty-eight years.

Gulls prefer to stay where the weather is warm but not very hot. So most groups have two homes. They move from their winter home in the spring, and they move back again in the fall.

During the spring and summer, many groups live in the kinds of places people go for their vacations. Herring Gulls may summer on the coast of New England. Ring-billed Gulls may settle beside the Great Lakes. Other gulls, such as the Kittiwake, go much farther north, to Alaska or Siberia.

When fall comes, the weather turns cold. Food becomes scarce. Insects die out. Rabbits and moles are harder to find. There are no seeds or birds' eggs to eat. Lakes and streams and perhaps even the ocean freeze over. The fish are hidden underneath the ice.

The gulls are forced to leave. The Herring and Ring-billed Gulls fly south to the West Indies or to

*Ring-billed Gulls fly over Mohawk Island in Lake Erie.*

*Distinctively patterned feathers mark a Bonaparte's Gull.*

Mexico. The Kittiwakes move south to the coast of Japan or California. There the weather is warmer and food is plentiful.

The gulls stay in their winter homes until spring returns. Then they return north to their summer homes to lay their eggs. This process of moving from one home to another is called migrating. Often the journeys are well over a thousand miles long.

Gulls fly at a speed of about forty to fifty miles an hour when they are migrating. Usually the trip takes two or three days of nonstop flying, and large numbers of the birds are lost during the flight. Many of those lost are less than a year old, and are making their first long journey; others are those members of the group that have grown old and weak.

The unlucky ones may crash into mountains in a heavy fog or in high, stormy winds. They may get blown out to sea. Or they may simply drop to the ground because they are too tired to fly any farther. However, most of the gulls do reach their destination.

They know where they are heading. Every year, each group returns to the same place. Many gulls can even remember the exact spot where they laid their eggs the year before. They alight within a few yards of their old nest.

St. Athanasius' School
Mountain View, Calif. 94041

A few weeks after they arrive, the female gulls lay their eggs. After twenty to thirty days, the eggs hatch out into chicks. This all takes place in the gulls' summer home. So it is known as the breeding ground.

The gulls have many enemies to guard against. Foxes and dogs and humans are all dangerous. So are big powerful birds such as eagles and hawks. At any moment they may sweep down on the eggs without warning.

Even when the eggs have hatched, the danger is not over. For four to six weeks a young chick is almost helpless. It cannot fly. Nor can it run fast enough to escape from its enemies. It is likely to be caught and killed by any predator who happens to see it.

Gulls therefore pick breeding grounds which are out of the way and hard for possible enemies to reach. One group of the birds may settle on a patch of marshland surrounded by high weeds. Another may pick a lonely stretch of sand. A third may settle on an island.

Gulls are safest if they are hidden from danger coming from the skies, if they nest where the dreaded

*Hawks may prey on young gulls. Here, a red-tailed hawk has caught a kangaroo rat.*

*A bald eagle speeds toward its prey.*

hawks and eagles can't see them. Many groups settle on the underside of a steep cliff. Generally, gulls pick a breeding ground where they will be by themselves. But some species, such as Glaucous and Western gulls, build nests close to each other. They may also build nests close to terns, pelicans, cormorants, and other kinds of seabirds.

When they return to the breeding ground, gulls approach it with great care. For enemies may have found it and be lying in wait. The gulls do not land at once. Instead they fly in circles around their home. They are searching for possible intruders.

For days the group keeps returning, searching for danger. At last, one especially brave bird touches down. He seems to feel very unsafe and keeps turning his head in all directions. He stays on the ground for only a few minutes. Then he rejoins the group, and all the gulls fly away. But the big step has been taken. When the gulls next return, they come to stay.

Despite all the gulls' care, enemies do find their way to the breeding ground. If a dog happens to wander in, the first gull who catches sight of it gives a special cry. It is an alarm call, warning of danger. As soon as the other gulls hear the cry, they leave their nests and take to the air.

They may just fly far enough away to be safe, but sometimes they try to drive the intruder away. One after another, they dive low over the dog's head, like bombing planes diving over a ship. The gulls usually are not able to injure the dog. But the attacks are likely to disturb him. If the gulls are lucky, he will turn and leave.

The members of the group may band together against outside enemies. But they are not friendly to each other. They steal and eat each other's eggs whenever they can. The males are especially quarrelsome and often get into fights.

However, every adult gull does have one close companion. That is its mate. Gulls begin to pick their mates very soon after they arrive at the breeding ground. Many were mates the year before. During the winter they drifted apart. At the breeding ground, they come together again.

This happens every year. For gulls are like married couples who stay together. Once two gulls have become mates, they remain mates until one dies.

Each pair of gulls occupies its own piece of land on the breeding ground. It is called a territory. The two gulls will defend it against any other gulls.

*Gulls stay with the same mate for life.*

Some gulls in the group are younger and have never had mates. Gulls do not mate until they are three years old. Soon the three-year-olds will also find mates. Then they, too, settle on their territories.

Gulls get along well with their mates. The male bird has a special way of showing his fondness. He brings food home for the female. He has already swallowed the food and half digested it. When he returns to the breeding ground, he chokes the food up from his stomach and out of his bill. Then the female swallows it.

Mates can easily pick each other out from the rest of the group. Perhaps they can recognize each other's faces, but they rely more on sound. A male gull may be asleep when several members of the group return to the breeding ground. They make a lot of noise but the sleeping gull doesn't awaken. Then his mate returns. She may give only one soft call, but the sleeping gull immediately wakes up.

Mates have good reason to get along well. They must work together to raise and protect their chicks. First, they have to build a nest where the female will lay her eggs. Then the mother and father must take turns sitting on the eggs to protect them. When the chicks hatch, the parents must bring them food.

*Five Great Blackbacked Gulls go on a family outing.*

But every day the chicks grow stronger. When the weather turns cold, they are three or four months old. By now they can fly well. They are ready to join their parents on the long flight to the group's winter home. Next year, the group will return to the breeding ground, and a new set of chicks will be born.

*A Herring Gull's nest contains three eggs.*

*Herring Gull chicks await their parents and food.*

*Young chicks, like their parents, have distinctive coloring. This one is a Great Blackbacked Gull.*

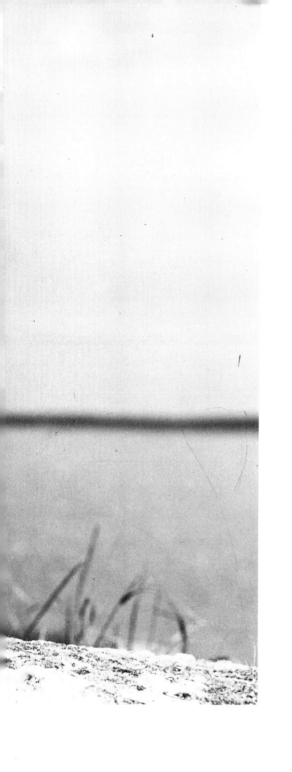

# PART TWO

*Gulls recognize their own mates or chicks by their voices.*

It is not easy for humans to understand why gulls behave as they do. We may not always realize it, but almost everything we do is based on thought. Suppose you spend an afternoon at a movie. You don't just find yourself sitting in a movie house. You must make a decision to go there, and that means you must think and plan.

Moreover, we have to learn to enjoy movies. For we are not born knowing how to enjoy them. Actually, we humans know very little when we are born. We have to learn what kinds of food we can eat, and how to get along with people, and how to obtain all the things we need to survive.

Gulls learn very little. They do not look ahead. They never think or plan, as humans do. Indeed, so far as we know, they do not think at all. Yet they often behave as if they do. For usually they perform just the actions that are most useful at any particular time. They leave their breeding ground and fly to a warmer home when food begins to run short. They return to the breeding ground in spring, when there is food to eat. They build their nests just in time for the female to lay her eggs there. And gull parents always carry enough food back to the nest to feed their chicks.

If gulls do not think, how do they manage to perform just the actions needed to keep them alive? The answer is that they are born with the necessary knowledge. They are born with certain drives which make them behave in certain ways.

This kind of drive is often called an instinct. It is the same kind of drive that makes a cat arch its back, flatten its ears and hiss during a fight. For a cat doesn't deliberately make up its mind to behave this way. It really has no choice. It arches its back because reacting in this way to danger is part of being a cat.

Gulls are driven by instincts, too. One kind of gull may be bigger than another, or have different coloring. But all the various kinds of gulls are born with similar instincts. That is why they all behave so much alike.

When the weather grows warm in early spring, gulls begin to grow uneasy in their winter homes. Day by day the uneasiness increases, until finally the whole group is driven to move. By instinct, every gull in the group heads for the breeding ground far to the north.

Once there, they all feel the drive to form into pairs. They pick their mates, too, by obeying their instincts. Usually it is the female who makes the first move. For instance, the female Herring Gull picks out one male and walks round and round him. Occasionally she tosses her head. The male may ignore her. If he does, the female goes off and starts to walk around another male.

But suppose the first male wants to mate with the female. He may join her and walk by her side. Together the two will start to scrape the ground with their feet. This is the way gulls start to build a nest. The scraping is a sign that they want to mate.

*Gulls perform courtship rituals or "dances" when they are selecting a mate.*

Or the male may respond to the female by twisting and turning his neck. He is trying to cough up food for the female to eat. She can see what is happening and she gets very excited. As the male coughs, she walks up and down in front of him. She may even grab hold of his bill with her own. At last he manages to cough up the food, and the female eagerly gobbles it down.

You might say that the foot scraping and the food

sharing are the gulls' wedding ceremony. When they are finished, the two birds are almost sure to pair up. Now they are ready to mate and have chicks.

Soon all the adult members of the group get the urge to build their nests. Together, each pair visits various places on their territory. They are looking for a place to build their nest, rather as newly married couples go looking for a house. Here and there the gulls stop and set about scraping the ground with their feet, as if to clear space for a nest. They also begin to hunt around for bits of straw and moss, and they bring these back in their beaks.

At first the building does not get very far; soon the two gulls move away and start scraping somewhere else. But day by day the drive to build grows stronger. It becomes especially strong in the male, who does most of the work. Each time he starts building in a new place, he carries the building a little further. Finally he gathers a really big heap of material in one spot. That is where the nest will actually be built.

In addition to straw and moss, the gulls collect twigs and weeds. They even pick up pieces of paper or string dropped by humans. When all the pieces have been laid together, the male and female take turns sitting on the nest. They do a lot of turning around, and this gives the nest a circular shape. When it is finished, the female has a neat and comfortable home in which to lay her eggs.

Usually she lays three. She lays them one at a time, at two-day intervals. Some gull eggs are almost white in color. But most of them are brownish with spots of black, brown or purple. The act of laying the eggs causes a big change in the parents' lives. Before, the two gulls stayed together almost all the time. Early each day, they left the breeding ground to look for food. Each evening they came back together.

But once the eggs are laid, one parent must always

stay with them. So the mother and father take turns. While one goes off to hunt for food, the other stays home.

The parents' most important task is keeping the eggs warm. This is called "brooding" and it is vital. If the eggs are not kept warm, the chicks won't grow inside them. A gull's body is almost entirely covered with feathers. But every adult has three featherless patches—called brooding patches—underneath its body. A parent gull keeps its eggs warm by fitting its brooding patches over them. Before it sits down, the parent performs a little dance. It lifts first one leg and then the other, swinging its body from side to side as it stands over the eggs. Then it gently lowers itself so that each egg fits into a brooding patch, right next to the parent's warm body.

A gull's drive to brood its eggs is very strong and it produces some strange results. The longer a gull sits on the eggs, the weaker its brooding drive becomes. By the time its mate appears, the gull is glad to get off the eggs. But the other gull has been away from the eggs for several hours, so it feels a strong drive to sit on them—and the two parents gladly change places.

Things do not always go so smoothly. Suppose the

father returns early. He may feel a strong drive to sit on the eggs. But the mother's drive is not yet exhausted. So she refuses to move. This situation shows just how instinct works. If two humans disagree, they can talk over their problem and try to solve it. But gulls can't talk. Nor can they think, as we do. They don't realize they have a problem. All they can do is behave as their instincts command.

The father becomes very upset and frustrated. He may even try to push his mate off the eggs by force. More often he shows his frustration in what looks like a very strange way. He goes off and collects a lot of straw and moss, and piles it around the top of the nest. A gull father may do this several times while the eggs are being brooded. So a gull's nest often ends up two or three times as big as the normal size.

Obviously the gull father is doing one thing when he really wants to do another. This is called displacement. It may seem very silly, especially when the father ends up performing such useless actions as adding material to a nest that is already complete. But other animals often do the same kind of thing, and so do we. Suppose you get excited while watching a football game. You may find yourself standing up and clapping your hands and shouting. Why?

*A Great Blackbacked Gull keeps a lookout over its chick.*

The reason is that you feel a strong drive to get down on the field and join in the game. You aren't able to do that, just as the father gull can't get to sit on the eggs. But your drive is so strong you feel you must do something. So you relieve your frustration by clapping and shouting and jumping up and down. Yet these actions are just as useless as the bits of straw that the father gull adds to the nest.

Parent gulls do not sit on their eggs the whole day round. But one or the other always stays near them to keep guard. Danger may come from the weather, perhaps from a heavy fall of rain. For rain can wash the soil and the nest away, and the eggs may be washed away as well. By squatting over the eggs, a parent gull keeps them from being swept off by the rain.

If the eggs are left unguarded for a single moment, another gull may swoop down and carry one off to take it back to his own nest to eat. Or the attack might come from an eagle or a hawk. Eagles are so big and strong that gulls are helpless against them. However, a gull parent may challenge a hawk. By itself, it can't drive the hawk away. But other gulls will often race to its aid, and the hawk will fly off.

Parent gulls do everything they can to protect

their eggs. They may even risk their lives, as in battles against hawks. Yet parent gulls can't tell the difference between their eggs and eggs laid by completely different kinds of birds. They can only remember where their nests are.

Of course, if nothing interferes, a gull will always find his own eggs there when he returns to his nest. But suppose somebody removes his eggs and puts others in their place? The parent gull will not notice that anything is wrong. He still obeys his drive to brood, or keep the eggs warm, and he and his mate will often sit on the strange eggs for several days. Gulls will even brood over a bit of wood or a small box. They have special trouble noticing the difference between their eggs and balls of the same size. Once a scientist put a golf ball into a gull's nest. The two parent gulls sat on it for more than a week.

After about a month, the chicks are ready to hatch out. They have to break out of their eggs by themselves. They manage it by moving slowly into an upright position inside the eggs, and then punching holes in the shell with their beaks.

A newborn chick is very small. He is only about as long as your first finger. He is always hungry and his first need is to obtain food. When he has broken

out of the eggshell, he starts to beg from whichever parent is closest. Suppose it is the father. Like all adult gulls, the father has a red spot on his bill. By instinct, the newborn chick reaches up and tries to touch that red spot with his own tiny bill. At the same time, he gives a thin little squeak.

*A Tern chick nestles under its parent's wing.*

The father can't resist this appeal, and he responds by choking up food. The idea of a chick eating food which his father has already swallowed might not sound very pleasant. But actually this method of feeding is necessary. For a newborn chick cannot digest raw food. But the father has already done most of the digesting before he coughs the food up, and the chick is then able to do whatever extra digesting is still necessary.

Newborn chicks are eager to move around. They stretch. They scratch their heads. They try to walk. At first they keep falling over, as human babies do when they first try to walk. But the chicks keep trying—and hard, for their survival may depend on how quickly they learn. Some enemy, such as a dog or a fox, might wander onto the breeding ground just after the chicks are born. He would have trouble seeing them. For newborn chicks are a kind of khaki or tan color which is hard to see against sand or grass. Moreover, dogs and foxes do not have very good eyesight.

Still, an intruder might stumble across a nest by accident. Even a day-old chick avoids this danger by another instinct. When an alarm call is given, and their parents leave the nests, the chicks try to follow, scattering away from each other. They can walk only a few yards. Then they crouch down and make themselves look as small as possible. Thus, the dog or fox has much less chance of finding several chicks together.

The chicks rapidly become more skillful at avoiding danger. After a few days, they respond directly to alarm calls. They no longer wait for their parents to move before they start to run for safety. They may even be out of the nest before their parents have moved. They still can't fly. But they can run quite far. They may hide under a bush. Or they may crouch deep in the grass. Or, when they are a little older, they may run down to a lake or stream and swim out to safety.

After four to six weeks, the chicks are able to fly. Until then they remain completely dependent on their parents. There is very little food in the breeding ground. So the parent gulls must feed their chicks. Every time the father or mother flies away, it brings food back to the nest. It is the father who brings the most, for he continues to cough up food for his mate. The mother and the chicks often get into squabbles over who is to get the food which the father has just coughed up.

Although parent gulls are not able to recognize their eggs, you'd think they could recognize their chicks. Yet for several days after a chick has hatched out, its parents can't distinguish it from other newborn chicks. Sometimes the parent of a very young chick will be sitting near his nest when a strange chick of the same age wanders past. Seeing an adult, the strange chick will probably come up and beg for food. The adult reacts exactly as he would if the chick were his own. He coughs up food, and the stranger chick eats it before wandering back to his own nest.

Like all gull instincts, this one helps gulls to survive. The parents of a newborn chick might be killed. If no other gulls will feed their chicks, then the chicks will die. But other gulls will feed them if the chicks come near their nests, and may even take the chicks in as their own.

However, parents do become able to recognize their chicks when they are about five days old. After that age, any chick that wanders onto a strange territory will be in trouble. The owners of the territory will chase it away. They may even peck at it, and this pecking can be so serious that the poor chick may be injured or killed.

These attacks are produced by yet another very strong gull instinct. Both females and males have a powerful drive to defend their territory against all strangers. The male is particularly determined. Suppose a male comes home and finds a strange gull on his territory. He immediately issues a challenge. He does so by walking up to the intruder with his neck stretched up and forward and his wings lifted. This position is a threat, like that of a man who is holding his fists up. It means that the male is ready to fight.

If the intruder is a female, she will immediately fly off. A male, too, will usually retreat from a strange territory when he is challenged. But he moves away more slowly than a female and his retreat may not be fast enough. Then the first male will chase after him, half running and half flying. This normally makes the intruder fly away.

However, male gulls often get into real fights over territory. Usually the fights break out between males who live next to each other. For each has the same strong drive to protect his territory, and this can easily lead to squabbles over where the boundary line should be.

In such a situation, neither of the males is ready to retreat. Both are determined to win the squabble.

But both would prefer to win without having to fight. So each male first tries to make his rival retreat by pretending to be very strong and tough.

Slowly the two draw closer until they are standing only about a foot apart. Then they gaze hard at each other, like two boys trying to stare each other down. Suddenly one gull picks at the ground and tears out a pile of grass or roots. The other male may pull out a similar pile, or he may seize hold of his opponent's pile with his bill and try to wrestle it away.

This pulling at grass or roots is, like the unnecessary nest-building of brooding gulls, another form of displacement. The two males may have a strong drive to fight. But they also have a strong drive to avoid the risk of getting hurt. So they compromise by trying to seem very brave and aggressive, without actually exchanging any blows.

Humans do just the same kind of thing. One boy may want to attack another boy, but is afraid to. So, instead of starting a fight, he calls the other boy names. Grownups are really behaving in the same way when they shout at each other.

However, male gulls are extremely aggressive creatures. If neither one is able to bluff the other into retreating, the bluffing soon turns into fighting. One of the males will walk up to the other and peck at him. Or he may seize hold of his rival's wing with his bill. Now the real fighting starts. The stronger male may grab the other gull's bill with his own, and drag him along the ground. Or he may force his rival off his feet. Standing over the fallen male, the victorious gull will peck at his beaten opponent with his bill, or beat him with his wings.

These fights can be very vicious and the loser can be badly hurt. Gulls are tough and ruthless when they are hunting for food, and they are just as ruthless when fighting. Indeed there are some gulls who seem to be natural bullies. Like boys who enjoy hurting smaller boys, these gulls deliberately pick fights with weaker members of the group and beat them up. And some gulls, like some humans, have the bad luck to be unpopular. These unlucky birds are likely to be continually picked on, attacked and beaten.

A gull seldom can change its position in its group. It can only behave as its instincts or drives command. In this, gulls are exactly like other birds. For all birds depend on their instincts to get food and to find mates, to avoid their enemies, and to raise and protect their chicks. Relying on instinct alone, they have been able to survive and prosper. The first humans came into existence less than one million years ago; there have been birds for about a hundred and fifty million years. The birds that are alive today are those whose ancestors were most successful in the battle to survive. Gulls are among the most successful of all. If they are left alone, they may still be flying over the beaches several million years from now.

# INDEX

*Note: Figures in italics indicate illustrations.*

PROPERTY

ST. NICHOLAS SCHOOL LIBRARY

LOS ALTOS